BE A GREAT ONE

Copyright 2025 by Steve L. Looten Sr.

Published April 2025
By Indies United Publishing House, LLC

Compiled by Steve L. Looten Sr.

This copyright covers the book, its format, cover, organization, and compilation and observations by the Compiler who assembled this book as a work for hire. No copyright claim is made to President Donald J Trump or any other pubic figure quoted in this compilation.

ISBN: 978-1-64456-806-4 [Paperback]
ISBN: 978-1-64456-807-1 [Kindle]
ISBN: 978-1-64456-808-8 [ePub]

Library of Congress Control Number: 2025903467

INDIES UNITED PUBLISHING HOUSE, LLC
P.O. BOX 3071
QUINCY, IL 62305-3071
www.indiesunited.net

FOREWORD

GLENN JACOBS

WWE Hall of Fame wrestler, "Kane"

Just about every political speech of 2024 dealt in one form or another with the future.

Any discussion about security, economy, jobs, trade, or health care all considered ways to make life in the United States better.

I believed Donald Trump, and certainly his team of advisors, provided the answers to offer us hope. This is why I enthusiastically support his efforts.

In my career in the ring, I quickly learned of the urgency for sacrifice and hard work to get ahead in life. I grew up in Missouri, and while I didn't have many major obstacles in reaching for my goals, I didn't have an easy journey either.

Mom and Dad made sure I was on the right path. They always made sure I heard what I needed to hear.

That is what excites me about this book, *"Be A Great One."*

We all can make improvements and strive for more success, but it's especially important for our youth to be encouraged to do so. I had to learn a lot of hard lessons along the way. I was tossed around in the ring for many years (and hurled a few bad guys myself,) but in my political career I've realized it also takes focus, teamwork and dedication to get things done, and it's never too late to start.

I've known the author, Steve Looten, for nearly 40 years. He was our sports TV guy back home in the middle of America and has seen many great victories and comebacks. This book may inspire more.

When he asked me to write this foreword for the book, he pointed out that I am the only person to know both Steve Looten and Donald Trump. Yes, my life is unique that way. One guy reported on how kids ARE great, while the other plans to Make America Great Again.

I have been blessed, and I hope Steve's book helps show the readers that from the great lessons learned in the 2024 campaign, their lives can be enriched and blessed, too.

I hope you enjoy "Be A Great One."

Maybe if it's a big seller, Steve's next book could be called "How I Survived My Time In The Ring With KANE."

Ding, Ding

INTRODUCTION

Inspiring Quotes from the 2024 Campaign, our History & Sports Champions

"History will judge us by the difference we make in the everyday lives of children." -- Nelson Mandela.

At times, planning for the future could refer to tomorrow, next week, next month, or even a few years ahead. When you're a kid, you might hear the phrase "save for the future" but that sounds like a hundred years away.

It seems like tomorrow will never come. But when you get older, you learn that the future knocks on your door soon enough. College tuition is an early slap in the face from reality, and bigger challenges are just a few more years ahead.

The youngest voters in the 2024 election were just ten years old when Donald Trump was elected the 45th president of the United States, and now they are already making a difference in today's world. Their future has arrived. This world will soon be theirs.

The Election of 2024 is their launching pad. Where do they go from here?

Nobody can benefit more from this election than today's youth. The life lessons shared by these candidates can pave the way for unbelievable successes for them, if they watch, listen, and learn. It's time for action.

In this book, we are reminded of an exciting future imagined by today's politicians, as well the words of champion athletes and other leaders who've learned to win. Their lessons can help shape the future for us all. In the 2024 campaign, new voices joined the discussion, and the future is exciting.

Their words may inspire greatness.

I am not an expert. I just love to tell stories about thrilling victories. I'm just a guy who loves this country and wants the best for our kids and future leaders. I am a sportscaster, and I just retired this year. I've always loved to talk about our area's conquering heroes, so you'll read plenty of great quotes from the sports world here. (I just can't stop it.) I believe sports provide the greatest reality TV of all. You win or lose. It's on you.

Honestly, the day after the election, regardless of who won, we all had to find a way to get out of bed, go to work or school, and live our best life. This time, Republicans won. More U.S. citizens believed what they had to say, and believed better days are ahead. In this book, we'll read the words that made a difference and gave us hope.

I greatly appreciate Glenn Jacobs' foreword. For a big bad dude from WWE, I've always known that he has a tremendous heart and cares about his family, community and country. Yes, he is a champion in many ways.

He was, and is, A Great One.

Inspiring Quotes From the
2024 Campaign, Our
History & Sports Champions

BE A GREAT ONE

COMPILED BY
STEVE L. LOOTEN SR.

INDIES UNITED PUBLISHING HOUSE, LLC

BE A GREAT ONE

CHAPTER ONE

GOLDEN AGE

"America's future will be bigger, better, bolder, richer, safer and stronger than it has ever been before." -- **Donald J. Trump**, elected 47th President of the United States

On Election Day, November 5, 2024, as votes were being counted in the close Presidential race, **Brit Hume**, Fox News Chief Political Analyst, said of Republican candidate Donald Trump, "He's the toughest son of a gun I've ever seen."

Trump had been knocked around and tested in every way since his first election in 2016. From day one, Washington Democrats were determined to ruin his reputation, get him thrown out of office, financially destroy Trump, and even throw him in jail.

But this seemed to energize Trump. He just wouldn't go

away, and certainly would not be eliminated. He seemed to be energized by the interference and seemed more determined to overcome it all. They say, "What doesn't kill you makes you stronger." Trump muscled up.

1:19 AM EST, November 6th, **Brett Baier,** Executive Editor of Fox News Channel's "Special Report," saw an image on his monitor, just as a nationwide audience saw it too. It was big news. Huge. "Is this a call, Ladies and Gentlemen? We are now projecting that Donald J. Trump will win the state of Pennsylvania. Former President Donald J. Trump will win the state of Pennsylvania, and thereby is on his way to becoming the 47th President of the United States." With Pennsylvania, Trump won that state's 19 electoral votes, pushing his total to 267, only three away from clinching the national victory.

Brett Baier: "In what is going to be the biggest political phoenix-from-the-ashes story that we have ever seen. Ever."

Trump was making history. Only once before had a President been elected back to the office after spending four years away from the job. Grover Clevland was the

22nd and 24th U.S. President, elected to return to the White House in 1892.

Martha MacCallum: Executive Editor and Anchor of Fox News Channel's "The Story with Martha MacCallum": "Grover Cleveland was not the subject of a Russia investigation, two impeachments, two assassination attempts, 91 indictments, convictions, and there is almost nothing that hasn't been thrown at this former president, and his tenacity in wanting to go back and run again."

1:46 AM **Brett Baier:** "The Fox News desk can now officially project that Donald Trump will become the 47th president of the United States."

1:47 AM **Martha MacCallum:** "The former president's comeback will be complete with a win in Wisconsin, a state that he narrowly lost four years ago."

With that announcement, the future had arrived. From Miami, Oklahoma to Miami, Florida, Americans worried about jobs, minimum wage, retirement, health care, immigration and the economy believed a fresh start was on the way. Promises were made.

2:28 AM EST **Donald J. Trump:** "Every citizen, I will fight for you, for your family and your future. Every single day I will be fighting for you with every breath in my body. I will not rest until we have delivered the strong, safe and prosperous America that our children deserve and that you deserve. This will truly be the Golden Age of America."

2:36 AM EST **JD Vance,** Candidate for Vice-President: "I think we just witnessed the greatest political comeback in the history of the United States of America. And, under President Trump's leadership, we're never going to stop fighting for you, for your dreams, for the future of your children."

2:52 AM EST **Donald J. Trump:** "America's future will be bigger, better, bolder, richer, safer and stronger than it has ever been before.

God Bless You, and God Bless America.

Thank you very much."

CHAPTER TWO

ENJOY THE CLIMB, AND TRY NOT TO SWEAT IT

"The struggles I'm facing
The chances I'm takin
Sometimes, might knock me down, but
No, I'm not breaking
I may not know it
But these are the moments, that
I'm gonna remember most, yeah
Just gotta keep going..."

--Songwriter **Jessi Alexander**

In 2008, I happened to be in Nashville, and a friend of mine recommended that I visit "The Bluebird Café." It's a magical place. Writers of many of Nashville's greatest hits sit in a circle, surrounded by about a hundred lucky audience members, and they play their hits. BIG hits.

I remember a writer named Wayne Kirkpatrick performed, and he was a writer on Eric Clapton's *"Change The World."* That song was for the soundtrack of the 1996 film *"Phenomenon,"* and was a big, big hit, winning the Grammy that year. Later in his career, Kirkpatrick wrote some monster hits for Little Big Town, including *"Boondocks"* and *"Little White Church."* He was part of the writing team that produced the soundtrack of the Broadway hit, *"Mrs. Doubtfire,"* and is currently working on a play about The Bluebird, itself. He was brilliant that night I was there.

I was at The Bluebird by myself, so they were able to squeeze me in at a small table right beside the talent. A very beautiful blonde singer was sitting no more than five feet from me. In fact, she placed her glass of water about two feet from me. Each of the four writers took turns singing their hits, when finally, one of them said, "Jessi, go ahead and tell them your news."

Jessi was Jessi Alexander. She said, "I was just asked to write a song for a new Disney movie. It's going to be for Miley Cyrus' movie called *"Hannah Montana, The Movie."* And then, close enough to "high five" me, Jessi played the guitar and performed "The Climb." I'm a big believer in finding ways to enjoy special moments in life. I really didn't do much this night, other than go to The Bluebird by myself. But there she was, an angel was *right there*, just four feet away, singing what would become a mega-hit. So, it's a favorite song of mine for special reasons. Whenever things seem difficult, I think of that night:

> *"There's always gonna be another mountain*
> *I'm always gonna wanna make it move*
> *Always gonna be an uphill battle*
> *Sometimes you're gonna have to lose*
> *Ain't about how fast I get there*
> *Ain't about what's waiting on the other side*
> *It's the climb."*

Of course, that song was a huge hit for Jessi, and it was a thrill to hear it about a year before the song and movie were released. She's become one of the industry's top writers, and now performs much more than before. (I could have given her that advice. She was magnificent!)

Now that I'm at retirement age, it's easy to look back and see how many moments and hurdles helped shape my climb. We all face that. Whether we're 16 years old or 60, we're going to face that climb. "Just gotta keep going…"

"Good habits formed at youth make all the difference."
-- **Aristotle**, Greek philosopher

According to Brookings, young adults quickly begin to worry about finances. They want to earn more than friends, more than older co-workers, and as much or more than their parents. And they want it now. Average credit card debt for Gen Z increased by approximately 14% from 2022 to 2023, and credit scores for young adults of color are even worse. In many cases, they're digging a financial hole as quickly as they can.

Brookings

https://www.brookings.edu/articles/how-economic-concerns-are-shaping-the-youth-vote-in-2024/

How can young adults prepare to avoid this? Owning that little house with a picket fence quickly seems impossible. Is this the American Dream, or its nightmare?

A CBS News/YouGov survey was conducted with a nationally representative sample of 2,460 U.S. adults interviewed June 17-21, 2024. In it, young people still had hope. Most believe they can make the dream come true. Most responders to the poll over 65 believe they already have lived it.

America's new generation gap: Young voters say they'll inherit a more challenging world. But will they vote in it? - CBS News

www.cbsnews.com/news/poll/-2024-election-new-generation-gap-young-voters-06-23-2024/

The American Dream was mentioned often in the 2024 campaign. Will U.S. workers be able to keep more of their earned income? Will prices of groceries be reduced? Will mortgage rates come down? Gasoline prices?

Vivek Ramaswami, at a Trump rally at Madison Square Gardens on October 27th: "We are happy to be part of something bigger than ourselves. You will get ahead because of your content of character and contributions. And I'll tell you something about my generation. We are lost. We are hungry to be part of something bigger than ourselves, yet we can't even answer what it means to be an American today."

"Answer, what does it mean to be an American in the

year 2024? It means we believe in the ideals of 1776. It means we believe in merit: that the best person gets the job regardless of their skin color, that you get ahead in this country not on the color of your skin, but on the content of your character and your contributions."

In the movie *"Field of Dreams,"* standing at a concession stand in Fenway Park, Ray Kinsella asks author Terrance Mann, "What do you want?" Mann, a man of great intellect and one-time voice of rebellious youth, answered, "I want them to stop looking at me for answers, begging me to speak again, write again, be a leader.' Kinsella glances over to the food counter, and said, "No, what do you *want*." Mann now understood, "Oh, a hot dog and a beer."

Maybe sometimes we try to make things too complicated. What do you want? What if we just focus on a good hot dog.

Findings of the "What Young People Want" survey conducted by the "Partnership for Maternal, Newborn & Child Health (PMNCH) indicate that education, skills and employment top the list. It's no surprise that young people worry about money, how to make it, save it, and how to gain additional education to get ahead.

The good news is that kids have time to change their course.

Education, skills and employment are the top youth demands World Economic Forum

www.weforum.org/stories/2023/08/global-youth-survey-skills-jobs/

"Take a deep breath." You hear that phrase, and there's certainly a lot to be gained by relaxing when possible and getting off the grind of life's merry-go-round. If your mind is always cranking at a hundred miles an hour, there's little opportunity for new, creative ideas to get in. I call it, "What do you think about when you're not thinkin' 'bout nothin.'" You've probably heard of people getting ideas when they're walking, listening to music, or taking a long bath.

Inventor and CEO of Tesla Motors **Elon Musk,** on Joe Rogan's podcast November 4th: "I mean, if I play a video game on extreme difficulty, then I have to concentrate fully on the game, and it has a calming effect. It sort of chills down. I mean, you mentioned, I think, many people, like if you play martial arts or you play pool, like something that forces you, it's like I think anything that forces you to concentrate fully actually has a calming effect. I find it just sort of like kind of a restoring effect. Like, it's good."

BE A GREAT ONE

CHAPTER THREE

GETTING INTO THE RING

"There are people a lot smarter, a lot more talented than I am, people who've accomplished things I can only imagine. Often, they started from the most humble of circumstances. That's my message: freedom and opportunity. That's the American Dream." -- **Kane**, (Glenn Jacobs) WWE Hall of Fame wrestler

Kane was as intimidating as any professional wrestler ever, but can you imagine that dude taking the court with his high school basketball team? Kane was somewhere between 6-7 and 7-feet tall, depending on which wrestler he had just slam-dunked to the mat. Known as Glenn Jacobs then, he starred at Bowling Green (Missouri) High School, and to his friends and family, was anything but a monster.

He was talented enough to play college ball, and that's where I first met the Gentle Giant. He played two years at Quincy College, then moved on to Northeast Missouri State University (now Truman State) in Kirksville, Missouri. If he got his hands on the ball, no opponent could really do anything about it. For nearly 30 years, he held the school's career field goal percentage record. He's still #3 on the list, making 224 of 395 for 56.7%. (If he had already created his wrestling mask, he'd have shot 100%! It's hard to play good defense when you're peeing yourself.)

His senior year, he even suited up for the Bulldog football team. As he contemplated his life after college, I interviewed Glenn about his life after sports. He wasn't done yet!

Glenn considered a tryout with the Chicago Bears, but a nagging knee injury prevented that. He surprised me when he said, "I'm thinking about trying professional wrestling." I thought he was nuts. I had never heard of anybody who made that leap. I couldn't imagine it. It's a good thing Glenn didn't rely on me to help fulfill his dreams. I couldn't see it. But Glenn could.

It's not easy, but Glenn was not going to be stopped. After years of hard work, he earned his big break. He put on that mask and became a superstar. "Kane dons the mask because he is horribly disfigured, unstable, mentally insane and crazy, so I thought it would basically look like he had escaped from an institution. Then, I get the creative work for the costume, and it looked like a superhero," he said.

"People ask what the advantages are of wearing a mask, and the first thing, of course, is the mystery - people don't know exactly what Kane is thinking," he once said.

Kane won championships and was on top of the wrestling world and a TV legend. He was one scary dude. And a star!

"People all the time come up and ask how we do this or how we do that, and there isn't any secret to it. You're just getting bashed with something, and you're either a man and you take it, or you're not. People don't realize the toughness of WWE superstars," he said.

In the middle of his popularity, Glenn returned to Bowling Green to sign autographs at a fundraiser at a local car dealership. The kids came from miles around, and Glenn greeted them in full costume, yet he remained in character throughout the event, not saying a word. He was enormous, and the kids were in awe. As I crept up to him to shoot some close video of Kane signing for the kids, I heard, from under the mask (so that only I could hear him), in his deep voice, "Hi Steve. How ya doing?" Nobody in the crowd could hear him, but it even thrilled a 30-some year-old sportscaster. He was still the same good guy.

Throughout the campaign for the 2024 Election, Donald Trump starting adding endorsements from mega stars of all kinds; wrestlers, fighters, boxers, singers, golfers and even other billionaires. His ties with fighters and wrestlers go way back.

"I'm a loyal person, man, and people who have been good to me in my life, I don't forget and I stand by them," -- **Dana White**, CEO of Ultimate Fighting Championship

"In 2001 my partners and I bought the UFC and it was considered a bloodsport. Nobody took us seriously. Nobody, except Donald Trump. Donald was the first guy who recognized the potential that we saw in the UFC and encouraged us to build our business. He hosted our first two events in his venue. He dealt with us personally. He got into the trenches with us, and he made a deal that worked for everyone. On top of that, he showed up for the fight on Saturday night and sat on the front row. Yeah, he's that guy. He shows up."

Brash and bold, Trump can be a loyal friend, and his enthusiasm for helping to build winners is contagious. Perhaps it is wise to surround ourselves with winners. Trump Plaza in Atlantic City hosted the main event, Wrestlemania, in 1988-89. Donald Trump was elected into the WWE Hall of Fame in 2011.

In January of 2024, Trump spotted invited guest Glenn Jacobs on the first row of his rally in Indianola, Iowa. Jacobs was six years into his term as mayor of Knox County, Tennessee. In recent years, he had learned to appreciate Trump more and more. They had hit it off.

"Another friend who's a friend of mine, another man I'm not going to mess around with…look at the size of this guy, man oh, man. He's all man. How tall ARE you? 6-8? What did you weight when you wrestled? About 300? That's not bad. I'm not that far away," and Trump laughed. "That's not good. You just ruined my day. 300?

"I guess there's a little acting involved, but when you

see these guys walking around the ring, lifting a 300-pound guy over his shoulders…it might be acting, but there aren't too many (who can do it.)… Then he throws him into the seats. It's pretty great. He's done a fantastic job as mayor."

Years ago, Kane and The Undertaker joined forces to create one of the all-time greatest draws in wrestling history, and this summer, they teamed up again. In October 2024, Glenn Jacobs and Mark Calaway (The Undertaker) reunited in a TV endorsement for Trump.

The fighting spirit is recognized by warriors.

Glenn Jacobs wanted a fighter back in the Oval office. He posted on X: "Joe Biden's incompetence is a danger to our nation and those fighting to protect it. We need a strong leader in Washington. We need @realDonaldTrump."

While the former president had opposition, in 2024 more and more people nationwide liked his tireless work ethic and were sold on his emphasis in making life better for the middle class. Whether Trump campaigned in Harlem, or inner-city Philadelphia, or Butler, Pennsylvania, people believed he was listening.

Perhaps it's true: People won't vote for you until they know you care.

JD VANCE, October 24, 2024 with Chris Cuomo on NewsNation: "I was very critical of Donald Trump in 2016 and I came around, because I probably bought into the idea that he was all about division in 2015 and 2016 and then I listened to what he said, and I saw the results, and I recognized that actually, the media story about Donald Trump is not always the full truth. In fact, it's often the exact opposite of the truth. So, when I go to a Donald Trump rally, what I hear is people from all walks of life. I hear people of all skin colors coming together, celebrating the country and talking about how we're going to redeliver prosperity in the United States of America. Again, I really do think that Donald Trump wakes up every day, and whether you're living in inner city, Detroit or rural Michigan, he thinks, how can I make your life better and more prosperous."

Dana White sees great leadership in the new President. "Anything can be changed. Anything can be fixed. Things that are broken can be fixed. And you don't have to be some billionaire or millionaire to do it. You just have to be a person with a vision and the passion to do it and be willing to fight for it every day." -- **Dana**

White

"The politician is your best friend - he always wants to be there when he's asking for your vote. But then, often, he doesn't have time for you when he gets into office. To me, it's the opposite. They should listen to you more when they're actually in office." -- **Glenn Jacobs**

Donald J. Trump, in an August 12th interview with Elon Musk: "We're going to give incentive to companies to come into our country, not to leave our country. We're going to be giving tremendous incentives. We want companies to build here, not to build in other locations. And we want to create jobs. And again, it's about the American dream."

JD VANCE, at a North Carolina rally: "Now I know a lot of us know young, young Americans, young families, our kids, our grandkids, and we just want them to be able to afford that American dream of homeownership."

Donald J Trump, August 12 Interview with Elon Musk: "You don't hear about the American dream anymore, Elon. You're the American dream in the truest sense, but you don't hear about the American dream anymore, and you're going to hear about it. People, they need that incentive to go out and do it. And they're going to love their lives. I mean, they're going to look forward to getting up in the morning and going to a job that they love, not a job that they can't stand, or not any job at all where they have no money."

It's a message that caught on. Most Americans want a chance for success. Was Trump the candidate who could deliver it? Time flies, and many Americans my age have seen a few difficult times but have also celebrated the very good ones. We want opportunities to be there for the next generations. Maybe there's another farm kid, like Glenn, out there with a dream.

"In the end, Kane will be remembered as a character I played on TV. In that respect, I want people to remember me for more than that." -- **Glenn Jacobs**

CHAPTER FOUR

WHATEVER YOU CHOOSE TO BE ...

"Keep away from people who try to belittle your ambitions. Small people always do that, but the really great make you feel that you, too, can become great." -- **Mark Twain**

I grew up on the same street as Mark Twain. It was Hill Street in Hannibal. Missouri. Hill Street started and stopped several times, and my part was a couple of big hills away, where I grew up right next door to the Mark Twain School playground. Talk about a field of dreams! It was perfect, because there were always baseball, basketball and football games with all my friends.

At night, my Dad would always sit out on our screened-in back porch, overlooking the playground, listening to the St. Louis Cardinal games with Harry Caray and Jack Buck on the call. Later, I heard stories about how Jack Buck was the finest emcee for many charitable events in St. Louis. He was a Hall of Fame broadcaster, but an even greater supporter of St. Louis organizations.

BE A GREAT ONE

I once heard him tell a group of students, "Whatever you choose to be in life, be a great one." What wonderful advice.

"Children are the living messages we send to a time we will not see."-- **John F. Kennedy**, 35th President of the United States

"Our children are the rock on which our future will be built, our greatest asset as a nation. They will be the leaders of our country, the creators of our national wealth, those who care for and protect our people." -- **Nelson Mandela**, former President of South Africa

"Every great dream begins with a dreamer. Always remember, you have within you the strength, the patience, and the passion to reach the stars to change the world." -- **Harriet Tubman**, American abolitionist and social activist

Hopefully hard, smart efforts can help dreams become time travel into our future. Golfers often step back behind the ball and visualize what the shot is supposed to look like. See it. Do it.

Dreams come in all sizes.

"We have every right to dream heroic dreams. Those who say that we are in a time when there are no heroes just don't know where to look. You can see heroes every day going in and out of factory gates. Others, a handful in number, produce enough food to feed all of us and then the world beyond. You meet heroes across a counter--and they are on both sides of that counter. There are entrepreneurs with faith in themselves and faith in an idea who create new jobs, new wealth and opportunity. They are individuals and families whose taxes support the Government and whose voluntary gifts support church, charity, culture, art, and education. Their patriotism is quiet but deep. Their values sustain our national life. -- **Ronald Reagan**, 40th President of the United States

"I have used the words "they" and "their" in speaking of these heroes. I could say "you" and "your" because I am addressing the heroes of whom I speak - you, the citizens of this blessed land. Your dreams, your hopes, your goals are going to be the dreams, the hopes, and the goals of this administration, so help me God." -- **Ronald Reagan**, First Inaugural Address, January 20, 1981

"All our dreams can come true, if we have the courage

to pursue them."-- **Walt Disney**, creator of Disney empire

"You must expect great things of yourself before you can do them" -- **Michael Jordan**, 6-time NBA champion with Chicago Bulls

"I just want to inspire young boys and young girls to be able to dream and do the same things that I have done. (And) I was just that young girl. I looked up to WNBA players, NBA players, college athletes, even other pro sport athletes. All you have to do is dream, work really hard, and be surrounded by really, really good people that believe in you, too." -- **Caitlyn Clark, WNBA star**

"If you want to succeed you should strike out on new paths rather than travel the worn paths of accepted success." -- **John D. Rockefeller**, American business magnate and philanthropist

JD Vance, in his acceptance speech at the Republican Convention: "I pledge to every American - no matter your party - I will give everything I have to serve you and to make this country a place where every dream you have for yourself, your family, and your country will be possible once again… But the American Dream that always counted most was not starting a business or becoming a senator or even being here with you fine people, it was becoming a good husband and a good dad, and of giving my family the things I never had as a kid. And that's the accomplishment I'm proudest of."

CHAPTER FIVE

EVERYTHING

"We have to abandon the idea that schooling is something restricted to youth. How can it be, in a world where half the things a man knows at 20 are no longer true at 40 - and half the things he knows at 40 hadn't been discovered when he was 20?" -- **Arthur C. Clarke**, British Science Fiction Writer

Throughout my life, I have been lucky enough to witness true greatness first-hand. Sometimes, it is planned, like when I went to see Paul McCartney perform. I just couldn't believe that I was seeing him with my own eyes. I had the same feeling when I enjoyed Billy Joel, Elton John, John Denver and Whitney Houston. Seeing Red Skelton perform was a thrill, too. Those people actually *created* all those masterpieces!

But sometimes you just stumble onto it. Right place,

right time, much like my Jessi Alexander experience. Those moments should be cherished. When I was in college in Kirksville, Missouri, I just happened to be walking through Baldwin Auditorium one night, and I heard beautiful piano music coming from inside the auditorium. I recognized the music but had no idea what the song titles were or who played it. After a great evening, I learned that it was legendary jazz pianist Dave Brubeck. That night, I slipped into the back row of the theater and watched his magic.

In 2018, I was lucky once again. My wife, Amy, and I were going to visit Rome, and a friend of a friend of a friend suggested that we contact a couple there for private tours. We had no idea how John Noronha would bless our lives. On our first day, John might have been qualifying us to compete in a cross-country event in the next Olympics. We thought our feet were going to fall off. There's a lot to see in Rome!

John took us from one amazing building to the next, highlighting the beautiful frescos, statues, and religious history. After about three hours of our first day, while he allowed us to try to suck in some air, I asked him, "How do you know all this?" He had amazed us all day long.

He replied, "Do you know the phrase, 'He knows a little bit about everything?' Well, my father taught me to know everything about everything. So, when I am on a bus, at an airport, on a plane or a taxi, I am listening or reading books."

It's been several years since our four days with John, and I still believe he is the smartest person I've ever talked to (although the guys in my coffee group all probably think they deserve the honor. Not no, but hell no.) We eventually learned that John was quite well known around Rome and the Vatican. It was as if we were touched by an angel. I think of his comment often: "Know everything about everything." I certainly don't have that hope, but the simple fact that John was motivated by his father's words opened my eyes. I had never heard of that idea before, or since. After that week in Rome, I would believe that John had completed that assignment.

I believe John's pursuit of knowledge had opened many doors for him. His opportunities seemed endless.

What might have been possible if I had heard that when I was 16, or 20, or 30, or 40? We're never too old to be curious. Knowledge opens up the world to us. Much like opening the gates to the Emerald City in the movie "*The Wizard of Oz*," knowledge provides the color to our life.

"The more that you read, the more things you will know, the more that you learn, the more places you'll go." -- **Dr. Seuss**, American author and cartoonist

Again, regardless of whether Republicans or Democrats are in office in the future, we all must find the color in our lives. Start painting. Create your own masterpiece.

"We need to think about how we teach working-class children about not just hard skills, like reading and mathematics, but also soft skills, like conflict resolution and financial management." -- **JD Vance**

"An investment in knowledge pays the best interest." -- **Benjamin Franklin**, founding father of the United States of America

Often, as we get older, we look back at our lives and wish we had learned more about our car engines, how to do more odd jobs around the house, learned more about finances (especially compound interest), and even learning how to cook.

BE A GREAT ONE

In a September 19, 2024, article called *"What Should Young People Get Really Good At?"* author Antonia Rudenstine, Ed. D., the founder and Executive Director of reDesign, writes that a 5-year-old's brain is magical.

https://www.gettingsmart.com/2024/09/19/what-should-young-people-get-really-good-at/

"They brim with questions: 'Why is the sky blue? Where do people go when they die? Why is my friend sad? Is today tomorrow? Who made the world?' (thanks to ChatGPT for this list). You find them wandering around playgrounds picking up rocks and sticks and buttons and glass to incorporate into their play. They tell stories and create drawings, sculptures, and paintings. They design games with complex scenarios and rules and experiment with objects in order to figure out how things work."

She continues: "In short, they are budding scientists, designers, philosophers, artists, and social scientists, engaged in refining future-ready skills. Their approach is transdisciplinary: their games and questions and design solutions are not limited to the knowledge and skills of science or math or ELA: they are building schemes that make connections that traverse the walls of our disciplines."

Rudenstine has made a career's work studying how to develop those young minds to maximize learning and creativity. How can learning communities enhance kids' experiences?

She suggests drilling down into the 2024 survey results to find that students report more engagement when the topic is something:

01. they want to learn more about
02. presented in an interesting way
03. learned in a hands-on way
04. useful in the real world; everyday life; a current or future job
05. that uses technology to support learning
06. challenging

There's just no question that change will continue to affect our lives daily. Her research reveals that "New careers are rapidly emerging, and many others will disappear in the coming decade: OECD predicts that 28% of current jobs are at the highest risk for automation due to AI and new tech (AI & Work, 2023). The World Economic Forum estimates that 23% of jobs are expected to change by 2027 (just 2 years from now), with 69 million new jobs created and 83 million eliminated (Future of Jobs, 2023)."

"Tell me and I forget. Teach me and I remember. Involve me and I learn." -- **Benjamin Franklin**

"I swear to God, if my kids, when they're 18, if they come to me and say, 'Dad, I love pumping gas. I love getting up in the morning, I love grabbing the handle, I love the smell of the gas station,' I'd say, 'Go for it,' because if you love it that much at 18, he's probably going to end up owning 25 gas stations by the time he's 30." -- **Dana White**

"Of course, we all come to the theatre with baggage. The baggage of our daily lives, the baggage of our problems, the baggage of our tragedies, the baggage of being tired. It doesn't matter what age you are. But if our hearts get opened and released -- well that is what theatre can do, and does sometimes, and everyone is thankful when that happens." -- **Venessa Redgrave**, actress

"There are three kinds of men. The one that learns by reading. The few who learn by observation. The rest of

them have to pee on the electric fence for themselves."
-- **Will Rogers**, American Vaudeville performer

We've all probably had one of those electric fence moments. I don't claim to be a genius and prove it often. Years ago, my wife and I, brother Rich, his wife, Kathy, cousin Jeff and his wife, Connie, took a cruise to the Caribbean. We were going to snorkel for the very first time. Of course, I never practiced, but I Googled "snorkel" once. That should have been enough, right? Reality hit me when the boat operator yelled, "Okay, jump in."

So, not having any idea if the water was six feet or 600 feet deep, we hit the water like those numbskulls on "Lifeguard Day" in the movie "*Caddyshack*." I quickly remembered that I was a mediocre swimmer, at best. BREATHE. BREATHE. I only had 30 minutes to gain some composure and figure this out.

The instructor said, "Hey, follow me. I want to show you something." So, a group of about twenty of us followed him further into the ocean. He had a small fish in his hand for bait and was going to go down to the bottom to a small cave to try to lure out an eel. This was going to be quite a show!

BE A GREAT ONE

As he waved his hand back and forth in front of the cave, slowly the eel emerged from the hole. As the guy backed away from the cave, the eel followed. The water was crystal clear, and it looked like we were in an aquarium. It was beautiful. It didn't take long for dozens of other fish to surround him, and when they did, he backed away.

When I could see again, everything was gone, except me, another guy, and the eel. It looked like it was about eight feet below me. *Directly* below. (It was probably 40 feet.) I realized I didn't know "everything about everything" about eels, but what I did know was that this wasn't a zoo. I was in his house! He was going to eat me.

I immediately took off for the boat. I was slapping water as fast as I could, and while I didn't know much about eels, I did know that I only had to swim faster than that other dude. Ended up, that was my cousin, Jeff. He didn't know anything about eels either. But we had a heck of a race back to the boat. The eel? Dead. Died laughing at us thinking we could outswim him, anyway. That day, I learned I didn't have to outswim an eel, just 'ol Baggy Britches next to me. We stared down that monster and lived to tell the story.

"Teach the children so it will not be necessary to teach the adults." -- **Abraham Lincoln**

My good friend, Mark Schlipman teamed up with Steve Short to write an excellent book called *"The Simple Road Toward Financial Freedom."* It truly is a guide to help readers learn the basics and develop a roadmap for successful futures. Imagine having this knowledge early! It's a great read.

They write, "It isn't so much a destination as it is a journey. It will require commitment, self-discipline, and delayed gratification – all internal skills that can be tough to master."

Doesn't this apply to many aspects of life? Commitment, Self-Discipline, Delayed Gratification – the steppingstones of life. Gathering knowledge helps us understand the value of the sacrifices.

"Small actions taken today can lead to amazing rewards in the future." -- **Mark Schlipman**, financial advisor

"We must educate and train our children to compete and succeed in the 21st century. Our kids are not going to grow up to compete with children in Alabama or

Mississippi. They're going to grow up to compete with kids in India, and China, all over the world; children who are learning to compete and succeed in the 21st century themselves." -- **Marco Rubio**, US Senator from Florida

Why let the magic of a 5-year-old fade away? Be curious. Ask questions. Ask, "Why?" "How?" "How Can This Be Simplified?" "How Can This Be Faster?" "How Can This Help More People?" Maybe we never need to lose our child-like enthusiasm. Maybe we can be fascinated by learning *almost* everything about everything.

CHAPTER SIX

RAISE YOUR FIST

Throughout history the job has asked
    Presidents to rise up and be great.
Often their courage had gone undiscovered
    until a crisis determines their fate.

Washington, Jefferson, & Honest Abe
    all faced their greatest fears
and calmly guided the country
    through some incredibly turbulent years.

When leadership is needed most
    these champions boldly stepped to the front
and gave America the spirit it needed –
    it's fight, it's heart, it's want.

Donald Trump wanted back in the job
    to repair this country's decline.
Forget retirement to Mar-A- Lago golf,

BE A GREAT ONE

    he's making the turn on D.C.'s "back nine."

He focused on the economy, security,
    and had a plan for more job creation.
Trump promised to make sweeping changes
    to jump-start prosperity for all the nation.

He had survived attacks in the courts
    and non-stop lies in the partisan press.
And he just kept rallying his troops.
    Together, they'd go clean up this mess.

But the cheering quickly stopped
    when the wanna-be assassin's shots were fired.
Mr. Trump was down. Mr. Trump was down!
    Nobody knew what had transpired.

Yes, he'd been hit, was bloodied
    and chaos ensued.
That's when we witnessed his determination.
    Oh, the stones on this dude!

Courage isn't needed until the only choice
    is to "do," not to "try."
From deep within his team of security
    Trump launched his fist up to the sky!

That's forever an image to remind us
    of the fight inside us all.
It's our modern day "Iwo Jima"
    when we're threatened, we stand up and stand tall.

As if to say, "Follow me. I'm not backing down.
    All together, we can win."
And the country bought in, then turned out.
    Donald Trump is President again.

Every president must deal with the unexpected. That's true in our daily lives, as well. It's important for young people to learn this early.

Boxer Mike Tyson once said that, "Everybody has a plan until they get punched in the mouth." Prior to election day, and since the day Donald Trump first decided to run for the presidency, he's been punched time and time again. But he's kept bouncing back. He's the greatest political counterpuncher in history. Again, in 2024, he answered the bell.

"Nothing comes easy. Success doesn't just drop on your lap. You have to go out and fight for it every day." -- **Dana White**

"Success isn't overnight. It's when everyday you get a little better than the day before. It all adds up." -- **Dwayne "The Rock" Johnson**, actor and former wrestler

"Life is full of surprises and serendipity. Being open to unexpected turns in the road is an important part of success. If you try to plan every step, you may miss those wonderful twists and turns. Just find your next adventure – do it well, enjoy it, and then, not now, think about what comes next." -- **Condoleezza Rice**, former United States Secretary of State

"Life is not about avoiding setbacks, but about how you rise above them. Stay focused, stay determined, and never let anything or anyone hold you back. Your strength and resilience will guide you towards greatness." -- **Caitlyn Clark**

JD Vance, at the Republican National Convention in Milwaukee: "Prior to running for president, he was one of the most successful businessmen in the world. He had everything anyone could ever want in a life. And yet, instead of choosing the easy path, he chose to endure abuse, slander, and persecution.

"But don't take my word for it, go and watch the video of a would-be assassin coming a quarter of an inch from taking his life. Consider the lies they told you about Donald Trump. And then look at the photo of him defiant – fist in the air."

Lara Trump, at the Republican National Convention in Milwaukee: "If Donald Trump has shown us anything, it's that when it feels impossible to keep going, those are the times we must keep going."

Donald J. Trump, at a rally in Milwaukee just days before the election: "We will never give in. We will never give up. We will never back down. We will never, ever surrender. We're going to start winning again. November 5th will be the most important day in the history of our country, and together, we will make America powerful again. We will make America wealthy again. We will make America healthy again. Thank you, RFK Jr. We will make America strong again. We will make America proud again. We will make America safe again, and we will make America great again. Thank you. Thank you very much, Wisconsin. God bless you. God bless you all. Thank you."

"I found that the men and women who got to the top were those who did the jobs they had in hand, with everything they had of energy and enthusiasm and hard work." -- **Harry S. Truman**, 33rd President of the United States

"Some people want it to happen, some wish it would happen, others make it happen." -- **Michael Jordan**

"Our greatest weakness lies in giving up. The most certain way to succeed is always to try just one more time." -- **Thomas A. Edison**, inventor

"If you get into something that you're passionate about, and if you really believe in it, you gotta get up every day and fight." -- **Dana White**

"I'm a great believer in luck and I find the harder I work, the more I have of it." -- **Thomas Jefferson**, 3rd President of the United States

"The amount of negativity I hear on a daily basis is unbelievable. But that's the kind of stuff you have to tune out, focus, stick with your vision and keep plugging every day." -- **Dana White**

"The test of success is not what you do when you are on

top. Success is how high you bounce when you hit the bottom." -- **George S. Patton**, U.S. Army General

"Hard times create strong men, Strong men create easy times, easy times create weak men, and weak men create hard times." -- **Vivek Ramaswamy** at the Liberty University Convocation, October 2, 2024

"I will love the light for it shows me the way, yet I endure the darkness because it shows me the stars." -- **Og Mandino**, author of *"The Greatest Salesman In The World"*

"If you hear a voice within you say you cannot paint, then by all means paint and that voice will be silenced." -- **Vincent van Gogh**, artist

CHAPTER SEVEN

AGAINST ALL ODDS

"If you had looked at my life when I was 14 years old and said, 'Well, what's going to happen to this kid?' you would have concluded that I would have struggled with what academics call upward mobility." -- **JD Vance**

We love a great underdog story. JD Vance told his story long before entering the political world. Throughout this book, we've highlighted great comeback stories in the sports world. I have been lucky to see many in real life.

Just about 30 miles from my home, I watched the 1997 Warsaw Wildcats boys basketball team rise up to make Illinois state basketball history. The Wildcats sure didn't look like champions. There wouldn't have been a lot of NIL money tossed at them, and pro scouts never knew where Warsaw was. The team featured a bunch of kids who might have bagged your groceries at night or raked your leaves on weekends. Heck, from the looks of these guys, on prom night you might have just waved them off the porch and said, "You kids stay out as late as you want." All-American kids, indeed.

They just loved to ball.

They knew where to pass the ball, where to set the pick, how to rebound, and they could "fill it up." I think the rest of the state of Illinois thought they were a nice little team, but not much more. A Peoria newspaper rated them 8th of the 8-team Class A tournament field.

In the quarterfinals in the big Peoria Civic Center, they stood tall. They handled Nokomis 64-51, to set up a semifinal matchup against powerful Chicago St. Francis de Sales. De Sales was *much* bigger, much taller, and might have been able to jump over most of the Wildcats, so it was no surprise that they jumped out to a quick lead. Then lightning struck.

With the final seconds running out in the first quarter, guard Bill Heisler, threw one in from ¾ court. As the ball sailed from one end of the court to the other, the team's hopes for greatness seemed to jump on for the ride! HE MADE IT! The crowd exploded. It was ON. Little Warsaw was ready for battle.

The Wildcats stunned de Sales, and advanced to the state championship game. And this spotlight shined even brighter. And new stars were born.

Warsaw and Spring Valley Hall had a shootout. Shawn Jepson of Spring Valley Hall scorched the nets for 52 points, but once again, Heisler was the star of the show. With time running out in the game, Warsaw trailed by 3, and the Wildcats pulled their next play right out of a movie script. Just like in *"Hoosiers,"* Heisler looked into the eyes of coach Jeff Dahl, and calmly said, "I'll make it." And let me tell you, seeing that play in real life was even greater than in the theater.

It seemed that half of the citizens of Spring Valley were trying to keep "Billy Ballgame" from getting the ball, but he fought his way through all the defenders, caught the ball beyond the top of the key, and BANG! The place was in a frenzy! Heisler ended up with 36, leading his team to an overtime win, and the Wildcats stunned the state fans! The celebration was crazy.

Several minutes later, I was in the Warsaw locker room

and senior guard Dan Buelt looked at me, his body exhausted, yet overjoyed, and asked me, "Mr. Looten, did you think we could do it?"

I laughed out loud. Of course I didn't. Nobody did.

Except the Wildcats. And they never had a doubt.

That is my favorite memory in sports. They KNEW. And they wouldn't be denied.

Sometimes you just can't accept failure. Perhaps that's what Vice-President Elect JD Vance felt. Who could have possibly seen greatness in little JD? But he knew, and it got him through some tough times.

In his book, "*Hillbilly Elegy: A Memoir of a Family and Culture in Crisis*," Vance describes growing up poor, with a struggling mother, and a no-nonsense grandmother, Memaw. When Memaw learned JD was hanging out with a kid involved in drugs, she threatened to run that guy over with her car. And when she died in 2005, they found 19 loaded guns in her home. She was ready for battle, too.

Yes, someone was looking out for JD -- Pistol Packin' Memaw.

BE A GREAT ONE

That was an early break for JD. Someone cared.

JD Vance, at the Republican National Convention: "I grew up in Middletown, Ohio, a small town where people spoke their minds, built with their hands, and loved their God, family, community, and country with their whole hearts.

But it was also a place that had been cast aside and forgotten by America's ruling class in Washington."

JD knew there was a better way to live and had to figure out how to get there.

I was still a sportscaster in 1997, and I was lucky enough to cover the 1997 Masters golf tournament. This is when Tiger Woods first looked like a legend in the making, winning the tournament by 12 strokes over Tom Kite. Throughout that weekend, the crowds grew and grew, and Tiger exploded as a star. After years of focus and preparation, he became "an overnight sensation."

Even he had his detractors. During the Saturday third round, as he walked from the 16th green to the 17th tee, it became obvious to me that his popularity was not unanimous. From within the crowd of hundreds, I heard one man quietly, but firmly, say that ONE WORD, yes, THAT word, and it proved that Tiger, and others would always face obstacles. I do not know if Tiger heard that word, I never heard anybody mention it. I suspect he heard it. I suspect that fueled his fire even more.

I also had no idea, that in his home in Ohio, young JD and Memaw were glued to the television, because Memaw *loved* Tiger.

JD Vance, in an interview, August 2016, with Terry Gross, on NPR broadcast "Fresh Air," about *"Hillbilly Elegy: A Memoir Of A Family and Culture in Crisis:"* "I was a very young kid, maybe 19 or 20, and the only reason my grandma was watching it was because he was in it. She loved Tiger Woods. And the reason she liked Tiger Woods is because she saw him as an outsider that was shaking up a rich man's game. And there was this really interesting moment where after he won - and The Masters always has this ceremonial winner's dinner to celebrate the victor. One of the golfers said something to the effect of, what are we going to have at the winner's dinner - fried chicken and watermelon, which, of course, was this extraordinarily nasty racist comment.

But it struck me at that moment, one, that fried chicken and watermelon was almost the cultural food of my people, and my grandma just got so viscerally angry. And she said, those a-holes, they're never going to let people like us be part of their crowd. And the sense that she had was they both looked down on the black people who were outsiders and the poor, white people who are outsiders. And she really saw the similarities. And that was the first real exposure that she felt some sort of kinship to people who looked very different from her but ultimately were similar in a lot of ways."

You never know where you can find inspiration. It could be by watching the "boy-next-door" playing basketball in a small town on the banks of the Mississippi River, or it could be watching golf on television with your grandma.

One thing is for sure, when opportunity knocks you want to be ready to answer the call. Put yourself in position to take, and make, the big shot.

"I went to college on the GI Bill after I enlisted in the Marine Corps and served in Iraq. And, so I stand here asking to be your vice president with extraordinary gratitude for this country, for the American dream that made it possible for me to live my dreams. And most importantly, I know that a lot of you are worried about the chaos in the world and the feeling that the American dream is unattainable." -- **JD Vance**, October 2, 2024 during the Vice-Presidential Debate

"We think of the Marine Corps as a military outfit, and of course it is, but for me, the U.S. Marine Corps was a four-year crash course in character education. It taught me how to make a bed, how to do laundry, how to wake up early, how to manage my finances. These are things my community didn't teach me." -- **JD Vance**

Vance used his experience in the Marine Corp to prepare him for college at Ohio State University. And he continued to work hard. He entered Yale Law School in 2010. Vance learned that hard work could pay off.

Now he plans to share his vision with the country.

CHAPTER EIGHT

ENDLESS OPPORTUNITIES

"A child is a person who is going to carry on what you have started ... He will assume control of your cities, states and nations. He is going to move in and take over your churches, schools, universities, and corporations ... The fate of humanity is in his hands." -- **Abraham Lincoln**

Today, it's easy to assume that all the good jobs are taken. Go to a local service club, and you see the bankers, business owners, and community leaders who are providing for their families. Yes, they're on their journey of success. But every year, workers retire from those good jobs, and some people move up the ladder, and others take their first step. There's constant movement, and the climb is easiest for those who prepare.

Every year, new opportunities are created. In a *Global*

Platforms article published October 7, 2020, called "A Better Future: Young People Have the Key," authors Johanna Diness and Gudrin Gadegaard Pedersen wrote, "The technological optimism comes from a generation of global youth which has actually seen a rapid change in the use and access to technology. In 2017, 2.7 billion people used smartphones, and in 2020, the number grew to 3.3 billion. In 2007, 20% of the world's population were internet users. By 2017, it had increased to almost half of the world's population – 49%.

Diness and Gadegaard Pedersen learned that technology can be a driver in a creative development led by youth, as one participant explained: "With new technologies we have more opportunities to do things differently than before. Increased knowledge makes people more aware of gender inequalities and can drive development. There is a rise in the number of young people taking action and are able to bring fresh ideas into the global economy, business world and educational sectors," and he concluded: "I believe that the young people have the keys for a better future."

Now, in 2024, we must have faith that exciting opportunities are on the way for us all. They always are, and anybody -- from those trying to make their JV team to those trying to be in the Senior Olympics -- can jump into the game, in business, the arts, medicine, education, and finance. If Donald Trump impressed you with talk about a "bigger and better" future, he should have. You are part of what can make America great again.

"Albert Einstein said, 'The mind that opens to a new idea never comes back to its original size." -- **Donald J. Trump,** in *"Think Like a Champion: An Informal Education In Business and Life"*

Since the election, Trump has surrounded himself with many of the brightest and most successful minds in the world. If he wants this country to "shoot for the stars," he might as well find someone who can build the rocket. "SpaceX is only 12 years old now. Between now and 2040, the company's lifespan will have tripled. If we have linear improvement in technology, as opposed to logarithmic, then we should have a significant base on Mars, perhaps with thousands or tens of thousands of people." -- **Elon Musk**

"Get going. Move forward. Aim High. Plan a takeoff. Don't just sit on the runway and hope someone will come along and push the airplane. It simply won't happen. Change your attitude and gain some altitude. Believe me, you'll love it up here." -- **Donald J. Trump**

"Faith gave me the belief that there was somebody looking out for me, that there was a hopeful future on the other side of all the things I was going through." -- **JD Vance**

"The future belongs to the dreamers, not to the critics. The future belongs to the people who follow their heart no matter what the critics say, because they truly believe in their vision." -- **Donald J. Trump**

"Let both sides seek to invoke the wonders of science instead of its terrors. Together let us explore the stars, conquer the deserts, eradicate disease, tap the ocean depths, and encourage the arts and commerce." -- **John F. Kennedy**

"Freedom is never more than one generation away from extinction. We didn't pass it to our children in the bloodstream. It must be fought for, protected, and handed on for them to do the same." -- **Ronald Reagan**

"A pessimist sees the difficulty in every opportunity; an

optimist sees the opportunity in every difficulty." -- **Winston Churchill**, former Prime Minister of the United Kingdom

"The more people tell you it's not possible, that it can't be done, the more you should be absolutely determined to prove them wrong. Treat the word 'impossible' as nothing more than motivation." -- **Donald J. Trump**

"Your work is going to fill a large part of your life, and the only way to be truly satisfied is to do what you believe is great work. And the only way to do great work is to love what you do. If you haven't found it yet, keep looking. Don't settle. As with all matters of the heart, you'll know when you find it." -- **Steve Jobs**, co-founder of Apple

"Shakespeare put it this way, in a famous quote from Julius Caesar: 'The fault is not in our stars, dear Brutus, but in ourselves.' That's a clear message. We are responsible for ourselves. We are responsible for our own luck. What an empowering thought! If you see responsibility as a bum deal, then you are not seeing it for what it really is - a great opportunity." -- **Donald J. Trump**, in *"Trump Never Give Up: How I Turned My Biggest Challenges into Success"*

A fundamental of journalism is to answer the questions: Who? What? When? Where? How?" Job searches can pose those same questions. For people wanting to find their big opportunity, consider the possibilities of the question, Where?

"It would be great if people returned to areas of the country that need talented people with good economic prospects. Our country would really benefit if those who went to elite universities, who started businesses, who started nonprofits, weren't just doing so on the coasts." -- **JD Vance**

CHAPTER NINE

YOU <u>ARE</u> SOMEBODY

"Failure is so important. We speak about success all the time. It is the ability to resist failure or use failure that often leads to greater success. I've met people who don't want to try for fear of failing." -- **J.K. Rowling**, author

We never stop dreaming of our future, and each step of our journey brings big questions. Who's my homecoming date? Where am I going to college? Where will I find my first job? Can I get a raise? My family is growing, so how can I earn a raise? Should I look for a new job? Will I ever be able to retire? Where did the time go?

Oh, boy, it goes by fast.

No matter what stage in life you are, you can take charge and start to take steps to do what you want and make what you want.

"No one is going to hand you the life you want. You're going to have to go out and get it…nothing happens if you're sitting on a couch waiting for your life to begin." -- **Dana Perino**, current co-host of The Five on Fox News, former Press Secretary for President George W. Bush

One key to a better life is to gather all the knowledge you can.

"One can best prepare themselves for the economic future by investing in your own education. If you study hard and learn at a young age, you will be in the best circumstances to secure your future." -- **Warren Buffett**, Chairperson of Berkshire Hathaway

How can you change your future in a big way?

01. Create an opportunity by improving an existing business or idea.
02. Create or invent a brand new product or service

"There's a good chance you can find success in one of your main interests. Explore it, learn it, master it and find a way to put your twist on it. If it can't be reduced, reused, repaired, rebuilt, refurbished, refinished, resold, recycled, or composted, then it should be restricted, redesigned, or removed from production." -- **Pete Seeger**, American folk singer

Focus on the first part of that statement. Whether you are a scientist, doctor, chef, plumber, electrician, teacher, contractor, waitress, small business owner, or nearly any type of worker, there are ways for you to grow. So, that sentence starts with "If it can't be reduced, reused, repaired, rebuilt, refurbished, refinished, resold, recycled, or composted," and those words can also be used to describe how you can look for ways for you to create your own business, if not improve your job performance.

In my hometown, we had a local business leader and community leader who said he first got involved in community causes when he thought, "Why doesn't somebody do something about that?"

He realized, "I AM somebody." Bob Mays lived into his 90's, and for decades never saw a community project he couldn't help.

In this discussion, why wait for somebody to create

these opportunities? You ARE somebody.

"The stars will never align, and the traffic lights of life will never all be green at the same time. The universe doesn't conspire against you, but it doesn't go out of its way to line up the pins either. Conditions are never perfect. 'Someday' is a disease that will take your dreams to the grave with you. Pro and con lists are just as bad. If it's important to you and you want to do it 'eventually,' just do it and correct course along the way." -- **Tim Ferriss**, author and entrepreneur

"If I were starting out now, I would look at what the competition is like in various fields--and then consider some that aren't so popular." -- **Julian Robertson**, founder, Tiger Management

"What do you need to start a business? Three simple things: know your product better than anyone, know your customer, and have a burning desire to succeed." -- **Dave Thomas**, founder of Wendy'

"Nothing works better than just improving your product." -- **Joel Spolsky**, co-founder of Stack Overflow

"Research how and why things are, and imagine how they might change," -- **Philip Anschutz**, entertainment mogul

"You can be creative in anything – in math, science, engineering, philosophy – as much as you can in music or in painting or in dance." -- **Sir Ken Robinson**, British author and orator

"Creativity is just connecting things. When you ask creative people how they did something, they feel a little guilty because they didn't really do it, they just saw something. It seemed obvious to them after a while. That's because they were able to connect experiences they've had and synthesize new things." -- **Steve Job**

"There is a fountain of youth: it is your mind, your talents, the creativity you bring to your life and the lives of people you love. When you learn to tap this source, you will truly have defeated age." -- **Sophia Loren**, legendary actre

"The American dream. Those three short, simple words encompass the hopes and aspirations of all the peoples on earth. The words are not only short and simple, they are also fragile." -- **Ross Perot**, businessman and independent Presidential candidate in 1996

"Establish a daily practice and use it as a way of getting through your days. Sometimes creative work really is just going through the motions. You don't necessarily need a vision. Stick to your practice, and things will appear. There's a Sex Pistols song with the lyric, 'Don't know what I want, but I know how to get it.' That's where I am. I don't have a grand vision for the future… but I have a practice, and I am curious to see what turns up, and that's why I get up in the morning." -- **Austin Kleon**, author, *Steal Like an Artist: 10 Things Nobody Told You About Being Creative*

www.serious eats.com
"How Bottled Water Became America's Most Popular Beverage,
March 7, 2023

Every year products come out that make you wonder, "Why didn't I think of that?" Although bottled water first occurred in 1622, it was only mildly popular until the early 1900s, when epidemics were caused by salmonella bacteria in drinking water supplies, and not until chlorine was added did it make a rebound.

But many older citizens don't remember bottled water in the 1970's and 80s. In fact, in the 1970s just 350 million gallons of bottled water were being sold in the United States – about a gallon and a half per person per year. By the 1990s, both Pepsi and Coca Cola had products on the shelves, and sales took off. By 2006, total sales topped 8 billion gallons.

Water. Who knew?

A glance back at the last ten years reveals some of the products that were introduced to our lifestyle. Somebody hatched these ideas!

Readers Digest, July 8, 2024
"19 Inventions That Have Changed The World in the Last Decade,"
by Elizabeth Yuko, July 8, 2024

- Artificial intelligence
- 3-D printing
- CRISPR
- Computer vision
- Internet of things (IoT)
- Apple IPad
- Cloud computing

- Video doorbell
- The Snoo Smart Sleeper
- Facial recognition technology
- Bioprinting
- Netflix streaming
- Semi-autonomous car
- Uber
- Instagram
- Air fryers

From Inc. com
"The 10 Greatest Inventions of the Past Decade,"
by Kevin J. Ryan, December 16, 2019

- Google assistant
- SpaceX's reusable rocket
- Venmo
- Nest thermostat
- iPad
- The self-driving car
- Consumer LED light bulb
- Ring doorbell
- Tesla powerwall

"Creative people need time to just sit around and do nothing. I get some of my best ideas when I'm bored, which is why I never take my shirts to the cleaners. I love ironing my shirts-it's so boring, I almost always get good ideas. If you're out of ideas, wash the dishes. Take really long walk. Stare at a spot on the wall for as long as you can. As the artist Maira Kalman says, 'Avoiding work is the way to focus my mind.'" -- **Austin Kleon**

What would be nice to have? Somebody is going to let their imagination run wild, perhaps while doing their ironing, and NAIL IT.

- Will somebody create a new way to get a good college education at a fraction of today's cost?
- Could somebody create a simple pothole filler?
- Is there some sort of electric fence to keep squirrels out of the yard?
- Will somebody figure out how to stop all hacking?
- Can we eliminate spam calls?
- Will somebody create a business where a computer/electronics expert comes to your house an advise you on all streaming/internet possibilities?

Now, let's read what some experts dream of.

"What Will Be Invented in Next Ten Years,"
in Forbes magazine:

"The discussions on technology were, inevitably, dominated by AI. There was consensus that no one really knows what's going on inside these machines and where it will lead. Even top AI executives acknowledge they aren't sure about the inner workings of large language models.

But what was clear is that the organizations getting real value out of AI today are those whose leaders are fully engaging with the technology rather than delegating it. Tinkering with ChatGPT for a few hours isn't enough. Leaders need to spend real time with AI. Ten hours will get you a basic exposure. Twenty hours will start to reveal some helpful use cases for you. And 30 hours will start to show you patterns of where you might go from here. Of course, the technology is improving rapidly, so you have to keep going back to stay abreast of its rapidly changing capabilities.

This is counterintuitive given the conventional wisdom that senior executives should focus on the big picture and avoid getting into the weeds. But it's not that simple: leaders need to know enough to gain intuition into how a technology will affect their business. The boss of a retail chain doesn't need to know every SKU code on the shelves, but they should be walking their stores on a regular basis to see what's happening on the ground. Similarly, CEOs don't have to write code, but they need to develop a strong intuition for what AI can do, and what it can't."

"What Will Be Invented in Next Ten Years,"
in Forbes magazine
Written by Dev Patnaik, CEO of future-focused strategy firm Jump Associates:

In an article on www.atlanticcouncil.org, authors Mary Kate Aylward, Peter Engelke, Uri Friedman, and Paul Kielstra wrote "This year, eight in ten respondents (81 percent) say that social media will, on balance, have a negative impact on global affairs over the coming ten years.

As for AI, despite a year of high-profile speculation about today's helpful chatbot becoming tomorrow's superintelligent force beyond human control, respondents feel reasonably good. Fifty-one percent believe that AI will have a somewhat or very positive effect on global affairs in the next decade, relative to 38 percent who say the opposite."

By atlanticcouncil.org
"Welcome to 2034
What the world could look like in ten years, according to 300 experts"
By Mary Kate Aylward, Peter Engelke, Uri Friedman, and Paul Kielstra

While we might not know exactly how AI is going to evolve, it is certain to be here to stay. In the 2024 campaign, 18-yaer-old Barron Trump used his life experiences to provide valuable advice to his father. Barron knew many podcasts that few on Trump's staff were familiar with, but the NYU freshmen knew how to speak the language of many previously out-of-reach voters. Barron recommended several podcasts, including the three-hour appearance on "The Joe Rogan Experience", which has had more than 52 million YouTube views. Democratic candidate Kamala Harris did not utilize advice like that.

Trump campaign senior advisor Jason Miller told the Politico *"Playbook Deep Dive,"* "Barron has been very involved in recommending a number of the podcasts that we should do. I got to tell you, hats off to the young man. Every single recommendation he's had has turned out to be absolute ratings gold that's broke the internet."

Today's college students now reading this book can make a similar impact. The future is now.

"One can best prepare themselves for the economic future by investing in your own education. If you study hard and learn at a young age, you will be in the best circumstances to secure your future." -- **Warren Buffett**

"The most reliable way to predict the future is to create it." -- **Abraham Lincoln**

"I think that the most important issue that will reshape our lives in the years ahead will be how man-made and artificial intelligence compete and work together." -- **Ray Dalio**, founder Bridgewater Associate

"I'd encourage more young people to apply their talents beyond finance and consulting and to think about reshaping how medicines are brought to market and how the business is run." -- **Vivek Ramaswamy**

"I really do encourage other manufacturers to bring

electric cars to market. It's a good thing, and they need to bring it to market and keep iterating and improving and make better and better electric cars, and that's what going to result in humanity achieving a sustainable transport future. I wish it was growing faster than it is." **-- Elon Musk**

All fishermen know that you don't make one cast and go home if you don't catch one on the first try. Bass fishermen cast and cast and cast, change lures, change locations and might even change their ballcaps. They don't expect to catch one every cast, but a few casts can make for a great day. Most highly successful businessmen failed often, until they didn't.

"You only have to do a few things right in your life so long as you don't do too many things wrong." -- **Warren Buffett**

"When you find an idea that you just can't stop thinking about, that's probably a good one to pursue." -- **Josh James**, CEO of Omniture

"Get five or six of your smartest friends in a room and ask them to rate your idea." -- **Mark Pincus**, CEO of Zynga

"The four most important words in business are, 'What do you think?" -- **Bill Marriott, Jr., chairman, Marriott International**

CHAPTER TEN

THE BEGINNING OF TOMORROW

"We should not look back unless it is to derive useful lessons from past errors, and for the purpose of profiting by dearly bought experience." -- **George Washington**, 1st President of the United States of America

We know more now than we did, but not what we will. All past Presidents handed off more knowledge to their successor than they took office with. Each President was faced with the "now," and made decisions based upon what they thought was best at the time.

Some major mistakes have been made, and those decisions hurt the country. But often the Presidents met the challenge, stood strong, and nailed it! Hail to the Chief!

Often, it is said in the sports world that practice makes

perfect, but legendary college basketball coach Bobby Knight believed in a higher standard. "Perfect practice makes perfect."

With our Presidents, while some have seemed to veer off course from time to time, generally they tried for "perfect" guidance again and again and again. Even in difficult times now, we have benefited from centuries of good intentions and vision. It is hopeful the Election of 2024 builds on that history.

After George Washington, each President added to the national record and discussion. Here are some of their thoughts:

2 JOHN ADAMS "Old minds are like old horses; you must exercise them if you wish to keep them in working order."

3 THOMAS JEFFERSON "Nothing can stop the man with the right mental attitude from achieving his goal; nothing on earth can help the man with the wrong mental attitude."

4 JAMES MADISON "Each generation should be made to bear the burden of its own wars, instead of carrying them on, at the expense of other generations."

5 JAMES MONROE "A little flattery will support a man through great fatigue."

6 JOHN QUINCY ADAMS "If your actions inspire others to dream more, learn more, do more, and become more, you are a leader."

7 ANDREW JACKSON "We are beginning a new era in our government. I cannot too strongly urge the necessity of a rigid economy and an inflexible determination not to enlarge the income beyond the real necessities of the government."

8 MARTIN VAN BUREN "There is a power in public opinion in this country - and I thank God for it: for it is the most honest and best of all powers - which will not tolerate an incompetent or unworthy man to hold in his weak or wicked hands the lives and fortunes of his fellow-citizens."

9 WILLIAM HENRY HARRISON "A decent and manly examination of the acts of government should not only be tolerated, but encouraged."

10 JOHN TYLER "Our form of government can no longer be considered an experiment in politics. Crowned with success, it stands forth an example to the world and exhibits the proudest triumph of reason and philosophy."

11 JAMES POLK "The whole frame of the Federal Constitution proves that the government which it creates was intended to be one of limited and specified powers."

12 ZACHARY TAYLOR "I believe in the power of the American Dream and the potential of every citizen."

13 MILLARD FILLMORE "May God save the country, for it is evident that the people will not."

14 FRANKLIN PIERCE "While men inhabiting different parts of this vast continent cannot be expected to hold the same opinions, they can unite in a common objective and sustain common principles."

15 JAMES BUCHANON "The ballot box is the surest arbiter of disputes among free men."

16 ABRAHAM LINCOLN "Stand with anybody that stands RIGHT. Stand with him while he is right and PART with him when he goes wrong."

17 ANDREW JOHNSON "The goal to strive for is a poor government but a rich people."

18 ULYSSES S. GRANT "... anything is better than indecision. We must decide. If I am wrong, we shall soon find out and can do the other thing. But not to decide wastes both time and money and may ruin everything."

19 RUTHERFORD B. HAYES "The progress of society is mainly the improvement in the condition of the workingmen of the world."

20 JAMES A. GARFIELD "Now more than ever the people are responsible for the character of their Congress. If that body be ignorant, reckless, and corrupt, it is because the people tolerate ignorance, recklessness, and corruption."

21 CHESTER A. ARTHUR "The extravagant expenditure of public money is an evil not to be measured by the value of that money to the people who are taxed for it."

22 GROVER CLEVELAND "It is said that the quality of recent immigration is undesirable. The time is quite within recent memory when the same thing was said of immigrants who, with their descendants, are now numbered among our best citizens."

23 BENJAMIN HARRISON "The indiscriminate denunciation of the rich is mischievous.... No poor man was ever made richer or happier by it. It is quite as illogical to despise a man because he is rich as because he is poor. Not what a man has, but what he is, settles his class. We cannot right matters by taking from one what he has honestly acquired to bestow upon another what he has not earned."

24 GROVER CLEVELAND "The ship of democracy, which has weathered all storms, may sink through the mutiny of those on board."

25 WILLIAM McKINLEY "The path of progress is seldom smooth. New things are often found hard to do. Our fathers found them so. We find them so. But are we not made better for the effort and sacrifice?"

26 **THEODORE ROOSEVELT** "It is not the critic who counts; not the man who points out how the strong man stumbles, or where the doer of deeds could have done them better. The credit belongs to the man who is actually in the arena, whose face is marred by dust and sweat and blood; who strives valiantly; who errs, who comes short again and again, because there is no effort without error and shortcoming; but who does actually strive to do the deeds; who knows great enthusiasms, the great devotions; who spends himself in a worthy cause; who at the best knows in the end the triumph of high achievement, and who at the worst, if he fails, at least fails while daring greatly, so that his place shall never be with those cold and timid souls who neither know victory nor defeat."

27 **WILLIAM HOWARD TAFT** "We must dare to be great; and we must realize that greatness is the fruit of toil and sacrifice and high courage."

28 **WOODROW WILSON** "I am a most unhappy man. I have unwittingly ruined my country. A great industrial nation is controlled by its system of credit. Our system of credit is concentrated. The growth of the nation, therefore, and all our activities are in the hands of a few men. We have come to be one of the worst ruled, one of the most completely controlled and dominated Governments in the civilized world - no longer a Government by free opinion, no longer a Government by conviction and the vote of the majority, but a Government by the opinion and duress of a small group of dominant men."

29 WARREN G. HARDING "The success of our popular government rests wholly upon the correct interpretation of the deliberate, intelligent, dependable popular will of America."

30 CALVIN COOLIDGE "Nothing in this world can take the place of persistence. Talent will not: nothing is more common than unsuccessful men with talent. Genius will not; unrewarded genius is almost a proverb. Education will not: the world is full of educated derelicts. Persistence and determination alone are omnipotent."

31 HERBERT HOOVER "Blessed are the young for they shall inherit the national debt."

32 FRANKLIN D. ROOSEVELT "Happiness lies in the joy of achievement and the thrill of creative effort."

33 HARRY S. TRUMAN "You can never get all the facts from just one newspaper, and unless you have all the facts, you cannot make proper judgements about what is going on."

34 DWIGHT D. EISENHOWER "Motivation is the art of getting people to do what you want them to do because they want to do it."

35 JOHN F. KENNEDY "Let us not seek the Republican answer or the Democratic answer, but the right answer. Let us not seek to fix the blame for the past. Let us accept our own responsibility for the future."

36 LYNDON B. JOHNSON "We did not choose to be the guardians of the gate, but there is no one else."

37 RICHARD NIXON "The greatness comes not when things go always good for you. But the greatness comes when you're really tested, when you take some knocks, some disappointments, when sadness comes. Because only if you've been in the deepest valley can you ever know how magnificent it is to be on the highest mountain."

38 GERALD FORD "The American dream does not come to those who fall asleep."

39 JIMMY CARTER "The best way to enhance freedom in other lands is to demonstrate here that our democratic system is worthy of emulation."

40 RONALD REAGAN "Each generation goes further than the generation preceding it because it stands on the shoulders of that generation. You will have opportunities beyond anything we've ever known."

41 GEORGE H. W. BUSH "The 'American Dream' means giving it your all, trying your hardest, accomplishing something. And then I'd add to that, giving something back. No definition of a successful life can do anything but include serving others."

42 BILL CLINTON "Our democracy must be not only the envy of the world but the engine of our own renewal. There is nothing wrong with America that cannot be cured by what is right with America."

43 GEORGE W. BUSH "America is a Nation with a

mission - and that mission comes from our most basic beliefs. We have no desire to dominate, no ambitions of empire. Our aim is a democratic peace - a peace founded upon the dignity and rights of every man and woman."

44 **BARACK OBAMA** "We need to internalize this idea of excellence. Not many folks spend a lot of time trying to be excellent."

45 **DONALD J. TRUMP** "I have made the tough decisions, always with an eye toward the bottom line. Perhaps it's time America was run like a business."

46 **JOE BIDEN** "But all our differences hardly measure up to the values we all hold in common."

47 **DONALD J. TRUMP** "Do not let anyone tell you it cannot be done. No challenge can match the heart and fight and spirit of America. We will not fail. Our country will thrive and prosper again."

It's interesting to realize that each President made powerful statements in their days, but in every case, they had to go to work again the next day and keep chugging along. In our lives, we must do the same.

BE A GREAT ONE

Today's problems need today's attention, and while the past may help us understand solutions, only a full understanding of what today's future appears to be will shape our thoughts, our needs, our solutions.

Today is today and is the beginning of tomorrow.

CHAPTER ELEVEN

WHAT MY GRANDPA WANTS ME TO REMEMBER

"If you can't fly, then run. If you can't run, then walk. And, if you can't walk, then crawl, but whatever you do, you have to keep moving forward." -- **Martin Luther King Jr.**, American Minister and activist

This is a solid life lesson, no matter what age you are. If you just graduated from college, it's not too late to find your passion. If you're closing in on your 50th birthday, your next jolt of energy might be just ahead. The famous un-sourced quote is, "No matter how long you have travelled in the wrong direction, you can always turn around."

"The secret to getting ahead, is getting started." -- **Mark Twain**, American writer and humorist

"I will prepare and someday my chance will come." --

BE A GREAT ONE

Abraham Lincoln

And as you prepare, you gather knowledge. Some of the best lessons are quite simple, yet highly meaningful. I call these ideas, "What My Grandpa Wants Me To Remember:"

- Pigs don't know pigs stink
- If you're going to do something, do it right
- I wasn't asleep, I was just resting my eyes
- That'll put hair on your chest
- How do you like them apples?
- He was drunk'er'n Cooter Brown (not life-altering, just makes me laugh)
- Don't believe anything you hear and only half of what you see
- It's always darkest before the dawn
- You may not be hitting it, but you're sure scaring the hell out of it
- Don't stare at the campfire, you won't have night vision if someone sneaks up on you
- Never lower your standards. Anyone who is worth it will rise to meet them
- Don't make someone a priority if you're only an option to them
- Never spend so much time in your life making a

living that you forget to make a life
- Life is like farming. Put in the work every day 'round the clock, And one day you will reap the harvest

And, of course:
- Somebody should do something about that. I am somebody.
- Whatever you choose to be in life, be a great one.

You've probably heard the phrase, "It's not how you win or lose, but how you play the game." Many strive to be a good neighbor, a good friend, a good teammate.

"All of us are born with certain gifts, and the secret to success is figuring out what your gift is and using it in a way that benefits others." -- **Glenn Jacobs**

"I've learned that people will forget what you said, people will forget what you did, but people will never forget how you made them feel." -- **Maya Angelou**, American memoirist and poet

"Get a job and when you earn a little bit of money, then you can do more good. Then bringing your values doesn't mean you have to compromise yourself. You got to get over this idea that you can't work for a big corporation, or for big oil or bigger pharma, because actually, those are where some of the great jobs are and you can do good there." -- **Dana Perino**

"I think that's the single best piece of advice: constantly think about how you could be doing things better and questioning yourself." -- **Elon Musk**

If it looks good, you'll see it. If it sounds good, you'll hear it. If it's marketed right, you'll buy it. But... If it's real... you'll feel it." -- **Kid Rock**, singer

Making adjustments in our life is often looked at as "What would I do differently?" College basketball great Jim Valvano was dying of cancer, when he reflected on life in a speech on March 4, *1993:*

"And when people say to me, 'How do you get through life?' Each day's the same thing. To me, there are three things we all should do every day. If we do this every day of our life, you're going to … Number one is laugh. You should laugh every day. Number two is think, you should spend some time in thought. And number three is you should have your emotions moved to tears.

Could be happiness or joy, but think about it, if you laugh, you think, and you cry, that's a full day. That's a heck of a day. You do that seven days a week, you're going to have something special."

Success is judged in many different ways. Certainly money is a major factor, but family, joy and friendship also are key. And they foster successful environments.

"I hear a lot of young people talking about the need to network. I think that is true, and I think that building a network makes sense. But I also think that there is another way to approach it, and that is to try to make friends. Just try to make a lot of friends." -- **Dana Perino**

"A bright future beckons. The onus is on us, through hard work, honesty and integrity, to reach for the stars." -- **Nelson Mandela**

"A country of tomorrow that will shape our future and reset expectations for the generations. And vision, a wonderful America, where the seeds of security, prosperity, and health are sown once again for benefit of our families." -- First Lady **Melania Trump**, in Madison Square Garden, October 28, 2024

BE A GREAT ONE

The fastest way to change yourself is to hang out with people who are already the way you want to be." -- **Reid Hoffman**, LinkedIn co-founder

"If you get up in the morning and think the future is going to be better, it is a bright day. Otherwise, it's not." -- **Elon Musk**

Be adventurous. The excitement of the anticipation of the next adventure is energizing. Learn to play the piano, guitar, paint, write, garden, walk, cook, travel, volunteer, remodel a house, take on a small role at your community theater, help feed the hungry.

Make it a point to compliment others, through hand-written notes, texts or social media.

Tip your waitress.

There's a great world out there. You're a blessing to others, and maybe today someone *needs* a little bit of you.

CHAPTER TWELVE

STARTING TODAY

"Let us charge together with a shared vision that builds on American greatness. Let's seize this moment and create a country for tomorrow, the future that we deserve." -- **Melania Trump** at Madison Square Garden, October 27, 2024

"Seize the moment." I've believed this all my life. This final chapter will discuss how being able to communicate well and being prepared for when opportunity knocks can enhance future success. Create opportunities for great memories and gather a heckuva collection of stories to tell someday, and many lessons in sports can help in the rest of your life.

In the TV business, I learned to always be prepared because you never knew when something newsworthy would spring up. Throughout my career, I was able to be the first camera on the scene to shoot video of car wrecks, fires and even a Mississippi River levee break, because my camera was ready.

BE A GREAT ONE

In 1992, I was thrilled to cover my first Masters golf tournament in Augusta, Georgia. It really is as spectacular as it appears on TV. Back then, I would shoot my stories during the daytime, then in the middle of the afternoon I would find a quiet spot, write my stories and record my audio so by 4:00PM I could Fed Ex the tape back to the station in Quincy. On my first day, that's exactly what I did, and then grabbed a new tape and a fresh battery JUST IN CASE.

I walked back toward the big oak tree where players gathered, and as I rounded the corner, "The King," Arnold Palmer, hopped out of his car to check-in. When he came back outside, he graciously gave me a one-on-one interview -- just me and him-- and my knees wobbled throughout our talk. I was ready, only because I made sure I had a fresh battery and a new tape loaded in the recorder. Always be ready for the opportunity long before it comes your way.

It's easier to see a shooting star if you look up at the stars once in a while. You never know when a star will fly your way.

On January 30,1999, I was lucky enough to cover Super Bowl XXXIV when the Rams' Mike Jones made a tackle at the one-yard line to secure their 23-16 win. That summer, the Rams had held their training camp about 70 miles from Quincy, so I had been covering the team all year. I was on the field shooting highlights of the game and was standing at the six-yard line on the game's final play.

Prior to the game, all photographers had been given very strict rules to get off the field immediately when the second quarter ended. They were serious. We were given only two minutes to scoot so they could frantically set up the big halftime show-pa-looza.

So, I did that as instructed, and hundreds of us were crowded into the hallways under the stands as they set the stage. I chose to get out of that crowd and walk down the hallway, and eventually I heard a big commotion from the other direction, so I walked down to see what the ruckus was all about. All performers of the halftime show had lined up outside the stadium and were now racing in from the parking lot and onto the field. I'm sure it was mostly dancers, but I felt as if the circus was sprinting by. My imagination in the last 25 years has convinced me that elephants, guys on stilts, girls twirling batons on fire, a yak, and maybe a few small carnival acts were part of that mad dash.

BE A GREAT ONE

There were only three people standing there with me watching this chaos. Then, back to my left, walking from the direction I had arrived from, two St. Louis Rams cheerleaders walked to us, past us, and on down the hall. As they crossed our path, one of the gentlemen looked at me, and raised just one eyebrow, and I got his message loud and clear. It was rock and roll legend Phil Collins, who was getting ready to perform. I had been standing next to him for ten minutes and didn't realize it. Communication often is the key to success. He and I shared that cheerleader "drive-by." He said nothing, but said it all. Eyebrow raised. Message received. There was something definitely "In the Air Tonight."

I've loved to find ways to create "Brush With Greatness" moments. In the business world, make being in the right place at the right time a practice.

When the Rams played their first game as a St. Louis team, they hosted the Chicago Bears on September 24, 1995, and legendary rock-and-roller Chuck Berry was the halftime performer. One thing was certain, I was going to interview him somehow, some way. So, after duck-walking across his centerfield stage, he bolted for his escape and I made my move. He ran from the stage to the wagon gate exit in the corner of the field, and I caught him midway. So, as he jogged, I ran backwards and got in a couple of questions. I have no idea what I asked or what he answered, but I cherish those 20 seconds of Q&A anyway.

Meet those people who can give you knowledge. Talk with those who've travelled your path before you. Learn to communicate *exactly* what you want to say. Learn to listen. And move your feet so you are where you need to be. Create a little fun for yourself.

As I was finishing this book, the 39th President of the United States, Jimmy Carter, passed away at the age of 100. He'll be remembered more for his life after the White House than during his term. He taught Sunday school for many years, helped build houses for the needy, and was generally considered to be a decent, kind man. Nearly 50 years ago, I saw him on the campaign trail.

I put on my "reporter's hat" when he was running for re-election in 1979. As part of his campaign, he took the Delta Queen riverboat down the Mississippi. I was in college at the time, and three of us from the staff of the Northeast Missouri staff of *The Index* decided to try to cover his stop in Hannibal, Missouri. It must have been

BE A GREAT ONE

95 degrees on August 23, 1979, and when the speeches were wrapped up, our editor, Deb "Beetle" Bailey, Larry Byars and I dashed out of there quicker than "Shoeless Joe from Hannibal MO." We climbed the steep incline of Hill Street to our car. From a block away, back down the hill, we could hear one man yelling loudly. We recognized ABC's Sam Donaldson, who was probably scrambling to beat a deadline. From our vantage point we could see an agitated Donaldson, and at the other end of the parking lot, we could also see who he was yelling at. Apparently, they had agreed to meet at the tall sign for the Mark Twain Dinette restaurant. They both thought they were in the correct spot, but Donaldson was on the wrong side of the building. I'll never forget hearing him yell, "I AM under the giant root beer mug!"

In the movie "Cool Hand Luke," a famous line described the root beer incident perfectly: "What we have here is a failure to communicate." Excellent communication skills will be a key in every phase of life. Your words mean exactly what you say, not more, not less.

Much like Phil Collins and Chuck Berry, our Presidents have often said much when saying little. Every word counts.

Who remembers, "The buck stops here," "Make America great again" and "Tear down this wall?"

The Trump 2024 campaign connected with voters with a clever, complete and optimistic campaign. It provided hope. Sometimes common sense is the best guide. Here are few campaign slogans NOT used, but maybe could have been:

01. Don't be a bonehead
02. Don't pee on my back and tell me it's raining
03. It's the economy, Stupid. (an oldie but a goodie)
04. Be a spreader of sunshine
05. Listen
06. Don't take people for granted
07. People can't (always) be bought
08. Even the little people are the big people

In October, I got to get a taste of the campaign action when I signed up to be a ballot chaser up in Wisconsin, as part of the Turning Point Action organization. I was assigned to Waukesha, Wisconsin, and was given 100 names to try to contact. I worked near Carroll University. I was up there for three days, about three weeks before the election. I know the organization contacted thousands of voters, but in reality, I cannot say I made a huge difference. It was difficult to reach my people during the day. I guess some people were working, the students were on campus, and many others lived inside large apartment buildings (or a couple of dorms) and those buildings secure from solicitors. I did not break those rules and respected their privacy.

But I did talk to some voters, and they were very interested in the election. I never really shared what my beliefs were, but I got people to tell me what they wanted, worried about and hoped for. They raised three topics most often: the economy, the safety of open borders, and how the Democrat candidate got the nomination. Later, I sent many postcards and texts reminding those on my list to vote, but I left Wisconsin unsure of what the November results would be. Although I told my friends back home that I had "saved the world," actually, I have no idea if I did any good at all. But, for the first time in my life, I was in the game.

Throughout this entire book, we've discussed taking that first step and enriching your life. This was just another experience to spice up my life. The status of our country in 2024 forced a lot of people nationwide to act and vote.

I recommend it. As the new administration develops new plans for our country, we're blessed that they're all stepping up. I also appreciate Americans from the other side of the aisle who also step up to work for what they believe in, and I believe more people will demand that we focus on our similarities. With many Americans promoting common goals, we can all benefit.

"He who is not courageous enough to take risks will accomplish nothing in life."-- **Muhammad Ali**, former heavyweight champion

"Tonight is a night of hope. A celebration of what America once was, and with God's grace, what it will soon be again. And it is a reminder of the sacred duty that we have to preserve the American experiment, to choose a new path for our children and grandchildren." -- **JD VANCE**, Vice-Presidential Nomination Speech, at the Republican National Convention in Milwaukee

"We don't have to be this nation in decline. We are still on our way up. We're still that country where we will look our children in the eye and mean it when we tell them, 'You get ahead in the United States with your own hard work, your own commitment, your own dedication, and that, you know what? You are free to speak your mind at every step of the way." -- **Vivek Ramaswami,** October 27 in Madison Square Garden

"Our freedom and future is in our hands." -- **Tulsi Gabbard,** October 27 in Madison Square Garden

"Now, I believe that we have the most beautiful country in the world. I meet people on the campaign trail who can't afford food but have the grace and generosity to ask me how I'm doing, and to tell me they're praying for my family. What that has taught me is that we have the greatest country, the most beautiful country, the most incredible people anywhere in the world. But they're not going to be able to achieve their full dreams with the broken leadership that we have in Washington. They're not going to be able to live their American dream if we do the same thing that we've been doing for the last three and a half years. We need change, we need a new direction, we need a president who has already done this once before and did it well." -- **JD Vance**, October 2, 2024, in the Vice-Presidential Debate

Much like the country, SOMEBODY must take charge of your future. You are somebody. You are the future, and Trump's acceptance speech on November 6th can be your gameplan, too.

"And every citizen, I will fight for you, for your family and your future. Every single day I will be fighting for you. And with every breath in my body, I will not rest until we have delivered the strong, safe and prosperous America that our children deserve and that you deserve. This will truly be the golden age of America. That's what we have to have." – **Donald J. Trump**, in his Acceptance Speech on Election night

Those words can be your rally cry. They can guide you as you continue your studies, join the workforce, to run a business, run a family, or run your personal life.

Fight for your success.
Fight for your safety.
Fight for your development.
Fight for your growth.
Fight.
Fight.
Fight.
Starting today.

ABOUT THE AUTHOR

Steve Looten, Sr. just reached the magical age of 65, when he should have all the answers. But that's not really the case.

Each step of the way, he's found that there seem to be more questions than answers. And he's learned to listen.

Most of his career was in front of the TV camera as a sportscaster on WGEM-TV in Quincy, IL. But occasionally he was able to volunteer for duty when presidential candidates came through town. In 1988, Mike Dukakis visited Quincy, and Steve served as the pool cameraman to follow the Democratic candidate through the streets of downtown. When Al Gore ran against George Bush in 2000, he cruised down the Mississippi, and again Steve volunteered to shoot video. As the Mark Twain Riverboat drifted into Hannibal, Missouri, from the north, Steve pointed out all the tourist sites to Al and Tipper Gore and Joe &

Hadassah Lieberman. "It was fun to point out the lighthouse up on the bluff, and the location of the famous white picket fence."

After 20 years in various local business positions, he returned to the sidelines in 2023 for one last hurrah. After a 23-year "vacation," he was lucky to "be a kid again," shooting highlights and telling those stories on TV.

This book quotes many highly successful leaders and politicians, but the heroes in his professional life were the local stars he covered who overcame adversity to achieve greatness. You may not have heard of them, but Michael Payne, Bruce Douglas, Amy Miller, Michael Washington, Rick Little, Drew Quinn, DeWella Holiday, the Ragar girls, Amber Law, Kirk Mosely, Tim Fischer, Terry Bussard, David Winslow, Kent Hackamack, Craig King, Bud Schrader, Larry Lunsford, Willard Sims, Kurt Warner, Sharlene Peter, Gus Traeder, Reno Pinkston, D.A. Weibring, Caren Kemner, Ben Daniel, Bill Connell, Ben Pitney, Norm Stewart, Loren Wallace, Don Foster, Steve Hawkins, Sherrill Hanks, Jerry Leggett, Diane Glaub, Gina Ensalaco, Mary Jane Johnson, Gregg Nesbitt, Beth Leisen, Dave Bennett, Jack Mackenzie, Fred Bouchard, Jim Unruh, Matt Long, Brad Dixon, Elijah Genenbacher, Owen Uppinghouse, Aneyas Williams,

Khloe Nicholson and Tom Lepper have shown extraordinary character seldom seen in the halls of Congress. THEY are the leaders Steve remembers most because he saw their special qualities in person. And there were hundreds more.

"I told their stories. And I loved seeing the future through their eyes. I hope our political giants can lead as well as these athletes and coaches I've known," Steve said.

"My wife, Amy, and Steve Jr. and Dan make every day special, and have given me a wonderful life. I hope everyone finds that kind of joy."

This book is an effort to encourage the readers to shoot for the stars and achieve great success. The 2024 Election revealed some courageous efforts by our leaders that can impact our lives for generations. But, it will be actions, not words that will define their greatness.

With education, motivation, determination and preparation for opportunity, we can all "Be A Great One."

www.ingramcontent.com/pod-product-compliance
Lightning Source LLC
Chambersburg PA
CBHW072212070526
44585CB00015B/1303